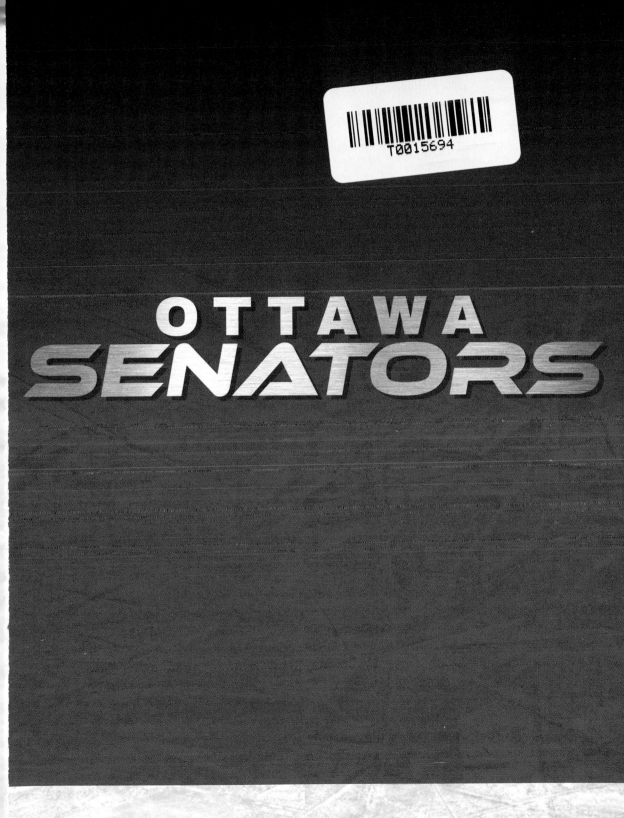

OTTAWA SENATORS

BY ETHAN OLSON

Book design by Maggie Villaume
Cover design by Maggie Villaume

Photographs ©: Nick Wass/AP Images, cover; Daniel Lea/Cal Sport Media/ZUMA Press/AP Images, 4–5; Adrian Wyld/The Canadian Press/AP Images, 7, 8; Gerry Broome/AP Images, 10–11; Jonathan Hayward/The Canadian Press/AP Images, 15, 16–17; John Hayes/AP Images, 13; Don Heupel/AP Images, 19; Chris Carlson/AP Images, 21; Winslow Townson/AP Images, 23; Steve Mitchell/AP Images, 24–25; Sean Kilpatrick/The Canadian Press/AP Images, 27; Justin Tang/The Canadian Press/AP Images, 29

Press Box Books, an imprint of Press Room Editions.

ISBN
978-1-63494-679-7 (library bound)
978-1-63494-703-9 (paperback)
978-1-63494-749-7 (epub)
978-1-63494-727-5 (hosted ebook)

Library of Congress Control Number: 2022919284

Distributed by North Star Editions, Inc.
2297 Waters Drive
Mendota Heights, MN 55120
www.northstareditions.com

Printed in the United States of America
Mankato, MN
082023

ABOUT THE AUTHOR
Ethan Olson is a sportswriter and editor based in Minneapolis.

TABLE OF CONTENTS

1

Jean-Gabriel
Pageau led the
Senators with
eight goals in the
2017 playoffs.

THE HONEY BADGER

The Ottawa Senators advanced to the second round of the 2017 playoffs. They opened the series with a 2–1 win over the New York Rangers. But in Game 2, the Senators' good feelings faded fast. The Rangers led 4–2 after two periods. The Senators needed to respond to keep their lead in the series.

Mark Stone gave the home fans in Ottawa something to cheer about in the third period. The right winger scored off a rebound to make it 4–3. However, Brady Skjei scored again for New York soon after. The Rangers were on their way to a win. Their lead remained with just over three minutes left in the game. Enter center Jean-Gabriel Pageau.

The "Honey Badger" redirected a shot from the blue line. That sent the puck past the New York goalie. It was Pageau's second goal of the game. The Senators still needed another one to stay alive.

With a minute left, Pageau placed himself in sight of the goal. A teammate sent in a hard shot. Pageau again deflected the puck into the net. It was

Ottawa's Mark Stone celebrates his third-period goal in Game 2 against the New York Rangers.

a hat trick. And the goal sent the game to overtime.

One overtime period wasn't enough. The game went into double overtime.

The Senators mob Pageau after his game-winning goal in Game 2 against the Rangers.

That's when Pageau led a two-on-one break. He had a teammate skating with him. But a New York defender cut off the passing lane. That gave Pageau a chance to shoot. He fired a wrist shot at the net. It flew past the goalie's glove for Pageau's fourth goal of the game.

The Ottawa crowd erupted as the Senators took a 2–0 series lead. They went on to win the series in six games. For the first time in 10 years, the Senators were back in the conference finals.

COTTON-EYED JOE

The Senators held a secret weapon during their 2017 playoff run. Anytime they needed a big goal, the DJ at Canadian Tire Centre cued up "Cotton-Eyed Joe." The Senators scored many big goals after the song blasted. That included Jean-Gabriel Pageau's comeback goals in Game 2 against the Rangers.

2

Daniel Alfredsson
played in Ottawa
for 17 of his
18 NHL seasons.

BACK IN OTTAWA

Ottawa, Ontario, had once been home to a team named the Senators. They were founded in 1883. And they played in the National Hockey League (NHL) from 1917 to 1934.

Professional hockey returned to Ottawa in the early 1990s. Owner Bruce Firestone had tried for years to get a team into the NHL. His work paid off. The Senators joined the league for the 1992–93 season.

The original Senators won the Stanley Cup 11 times. The new Senators had some big shoes to fill. And early on, they didn't fill them very well.

The Senators won only 10 games in 1992–93. That tied the NHL record for the fewest points in an 84-game season. The losing continued for three more seasons. Ottawa finished last in its division each year. That had its benefits, though.

MAJOR UPSET

The Senators played their first home game on October 8, 1992. More than 10,000 fans showed up to see Ottawa take on the powerful Montreal Canadiens. The Senators put four goals past Hall of Fame goalie Patrick Roy. They went on to win 5–3. The roles soon reversed. Ottawa ended the season as one of the worst teams in league history. The Canadiens went on to win the Stanley Cup that year.

Alexei Yashin (right) captained the Senators in the 1998–99 season.

The Senators were slowly building through
the draft. The team's first draft pick was
Alexei Yashin in 1992. He arrived in the
NHL in 1993–94. The 20-year-old center

led his team with 79 points. The Senators drafted other young talents in center Radek Bonk and right winger Daniel Alfredsson. They paired well with Yashin. However, the team continued to struggle.

By 1995–96, the Senators hadn't won more than 18 games in a season. During that season, ownership decided the team needed a new coach. They hired Jacques Martin. His defensive style helped Ottawa improve quickly. The Senators made the playoffs for the first time in Martin's first full season in 1996–97. They didn't go far in the playoffs. But things were turning around in Ottawa.

Radek Bonk (14) spent 10 seasons playing with the Senators.

3

Goalie Patrick Lalime won 146 of the 283 games he played with Ottawa.

TURNING TIDES

The Senators were back in the playoffs in 1998. And this time they found some success. Ottawa opened against the favored New Jersey Devils. The teams split the first two games. Then the Senators rolled to win the series in six games.

The run ended after that. But the team continued to improve under Jacques Martin. Making the playoffs became a habit.

In 1998–99, the Senators finished with 103 points. It was their first 100-point season. For his work, Martin was given the Jack Adams Award as the league's best coach.

The Senators continued to make the playoffs every year under Martin. The team even won the Presidents' Trophy in 2002–03. That goes to the team with the most points in the regular season. They made it to the conference finals in 2003. However, an early playoff exit followed in 2004. The team decided it needed to make a change in hopes of winning a Stanley Cup. The Senators fired Martin after eight straight playoff seasons.

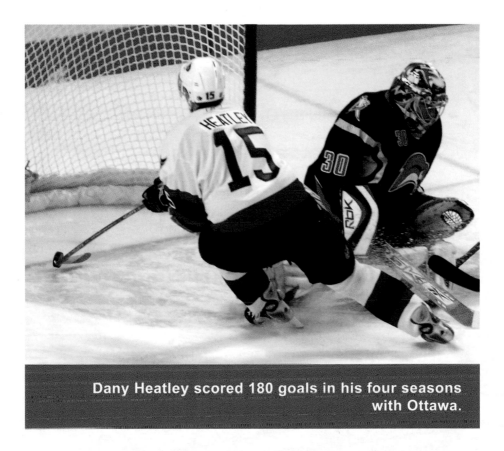

Dany Heatley scored 180 goals in his four seasons with Ottawa.

New head coach Bryan Murray kept the team competitive. The roster was still full of talent. Daniel Alfredsson was in his prime. So were defenseman Chris Phillips and left winger Dany Heatley.

And they were all at their best in Murray's second year.

The Senators rolled through the first two rounds of the 2007 playoffs. That brought up a showdown with the favored Buffalo Sabres in the conference finals. The Senators stayed dominant. It took them just five games to move past the Sabres. That sent the team to its first Stanley Cup Final.

FROM THE BENCH TO THE OFFICE

General manager (GM) John Muckler moved on from the Senators after the 2007 Stanley Cup Final appearance. Ownership wanted a replacement who already knew the team well. They chose Bryan Murray. He had coached the team for two years. He took over as GM and stayed in that role until 2016.

Ottawa fans celebrate inside Scotiabank Place after the Senators won Game 3 of the 2007 Stanley Cup Final.

The magic ended there against the Anaheim Ducks. Ottawa finally got its first win in Game 3. And even that required a late comeback. But that proved to be the high point. The Senators lost the Final 4–1.

DANIEL ALFREDSSON

The Senators picked Daniel Alfredsson in the sixth round of the 1994 draft. Many players selected so late never make the NHL. Alfredsson did that—and then some. The Swedish forward won the Calder Memorial Trophy in 1995–96. It's given to the best rookie in the league.

Alfredsson became a staple for the Senators. He was a consistent scorer. And he developed into the team's leader. Alfredsson spent 17 seasons with the Senators. That put his name all over the Ottawa record books. He retired in 2014 as the team's leader in points, goals, and assists.

Alfredsson was a key player during the best years in team history. That especially showed during the run to the 2007 Stanley Cup Final. Alfredsson's 14 goals and 22 points both led all players in the playoffs that year.

Daniel Alfredsson tallied 100
points in 121 playoff games
while playing with Ottawa.

4

Erik Karlsson captained the Senators from 2014–15 to 2017–18.

STILL SEARCHING

The Senators went through a rough patch after the 2007 playoff run. Dany Heatley was unhappy. The star winger demanded a trade. He got his wish after the 2008–09 season. Ottawa missed the playoffs that year. That snapped an 11-year playoff streak. By 2011, most of Ottawa's big stars had left. Captain Daniel Alfredsson was 38 and heading into his final years.

The 2011–12 season saw the Senators surprisingly make the playoffs. They lost in the first round to the New York Rangers. But it gave confidence to the young team. The Senators continued to change in 2013. Alfredsson signed with the Detroit Red Wings. The team shifted to build around star defenseman Erik Karlsson.

The Senators didn't get far in the playoffs again until 2017. The first round against the Boston Bruins went back

TAKING TRADITION OUTDOORS

In 2017, the Senators hosted the Montreal Canadiens in the NHL 100 Classic. It celebrated the 100th anniversary of the league. The game was played outside at TD Place Stadium in Ottawa. It marked Ottawa's first outdoor NHL game.

Fireworks shoot off before the NHL 100 Classic in 2017.

and forth. Left winger Clarke MacArthur's overtime goal in Game 6 won the series for Ottawa. The Senators then defeated the Rangers in the next round. Jean-Gabriel Pageau scored six goals in six games in that series.

The Senators met the Pittsburgh Penguins in the conference finals. No team had scored more goals that season than the Penguins. But the Senators shut down Pittsburgh's attack early in the series. It went all the way to Game 7. Only in double overtime did the Penguins finally knock out the Senators.

After that run, Ottawa began a streak of missing the playoffs. It was time to rebuild with young players. Talented left winger Brady Tkachuk started his career in Ottawa in 2018. And in 2021, he signed a long-term contract with the team. Fans in

Brady Tkachuk led the Senators with 67 points in the 2021–22 season.

Ottawa had high hopes that Tkachuk could make the Senators a consistent playoff team again.

• OTTAWA SENATORS
QUICK STATS

FOUNDED: 1992

STANLEY CUP CHAMPIONSHIPS: 0

KEY COACHES:

- Jacques Martin (1996–2004): 341 wins, 235 losses, 96 ties, 20 overtime losses

- Bryan Murray (2005–07, 2008): 107 wins, 55 losses, 20 overtime losses

- Paul MacLean (2011–14): 114 wins, 90 losses, 35 overtime losses

HOME ARENA: Canadian Tire Centre (Ottawa, ON)

MOST CAREER POINTS: Daniel Alfredsson (1,108)

MOST CAREER GOALS: Daniel Alfredsson (426)

MOST CAREER ASSISTS: Daniel Alfredsson (682)

MOST CAREER SHUTOUTS: Patrick Lalime (30)

Stats are accurate through the 2021–22 season.

GLOSSARY

CAPTAIN
A player who serves as the leader of a team.

DEFLECTED
When a shot is redirected with a stick or body part.

DRAFT
An event that allows teams to choose new players coming into a league.

OVERTIME
An additional period of play to decide a game's winner.

PRIME
An athlete's best years.

REBOUND
When the goalie makes a save, but the puck goes back into play.

ROOKIE
A first-year player.

SERIES
A number of games played between two teams in the playoffs.

• TO LEARN MORE

BOOKS

Davidson, B. Keith. *NHL*. New York: Crabtree Publishing, 2022.

Duling, Kaitlyn. *Women in Hockey*. Lake Elmo, MN: Focus Readers, 2020.

Hewson, Anthony K. *GOATs of Hockey*. Minneapolis: Abdo Publishing, 2022.

MORE INFORMATION

To learn more about the Ottawa Senators, go to **pressboxbooks.com/AllAccess**.

These links are routinely monitored and updated to provide the most current information available.

INDEX